20 Answers

God

Trent Horn

Catholic Answers Press

20 Answers: God

Trent Horn

© 2015 Catholic Answers

Published by Catholic Answers, Inc.
2020 Gillespie Way
El Cajon, California 92020
1-888-291-8000 orders
619-387-0042 fax
catholic.com

Printed in the United States of America

978-1-941663-65-3
978-1-941663-66-0 Kindle
978-1-941663-67-7 ePub

Introduction

"I don't believe in God any more than I believe in Santa Claus." Have you ever heard someone say something like this? I have. In fact, I have known several people who used to be religious but abandoned their faith because they felt they had "outgrown God."

But the thing they outgrew was not God. Instead it was a false conception of God—one that they may have even learned about in Sunday school. Their idea of God was, in the words of twentieth-century Bible scholar J.B. Phillips, "too small."

This booklet is an answer to anyone with that false, too-small idea of God: to those who say God doesn't exist or that he's just the universe; that God is a physical being like us; that God created the universe but doesn't care about it anymore.

In response to these views and others, I'll explain why Christians believe in the one true God, with evidence from reason, Sacred Scripture, and Sacred Tradition that gives us good reason to believe in the God who is, as the Athanasian Creed tells us, "one person of the Father, another of the Son, and another of the Holy Spirit . . . all one, the glory equal, the majesty coeternal."

1. What is God?

Although concepts of God differ across the world, they

all usually describe him as the supernatural creator of the universe. One useful but incomplete definition comes from the old *Baltimore Catechism*: "When we say that God is the Supreme Being we mean that he is above all creatures, the self-existing and infinitely perfect spirit. 'I am the first, and I am the last, and besides me there is no God (Is. 44:6).'"[1]

According to the Western philosophical tradition, God is *necessary* (he cannot fail to exist), *infinite* (without limit), *eternal* (not bound by time), *immaterial* (not bound by space), *omnipotent* (all-powerful), and *omniscient* (all-knowing). Finally, God is all-good: the perfect embodiment of the virtues of love, justice, and every other good we know. He is, as St. Anselm of Canterbury declared, the being "than which no greater can be thought."

Because God is infinitely beyond us, we can only understand him in indirect ways. We can know what God is *not*. For example: God exists beyond space so he is not made of matter (the stuff that occupies space). God is morally perfect so he does not sin. God is beyond time so he has no beginning or end.

When people try to define what God is, they often make the mistake of treating him like any other being in the universe, albeit one with unlimited attributes. But classical theists like St. Thomas Aquinas did not consider God to be one being among many (like a special star floating far away "out there"). Instead they considered God to *be* "being" or "existence" itself. What does that mean?

According to St. Thomas, in all creatures there is a difference between *what* they are (their essence) and the *fact that* they are (their existence). Just because something is a human or is a fish, for example, does not tell us if that particular thing, be it man or mackerel, has to exist. For example, there are many true statements that can be made about dinosaurs and their unique essence, but the statement that "dinosaurs exist" is not one of them, since dinosaurs went extinct millions of years ago.

God is different because his essence, or *what* he is, *is* existence. God doesn't just *happen* to exist like humans or other species on Earth; he *must* exist because he is existence itself. This is the meaning of God's name "I AM" that was revealed to Moses in the burning bush (Exod. 3:14).

The *Catechism of the Catholic Church* (CCC) explains it this way:

> The revelation of the ineffable name "I AM WHO AM" contains then the truth that God alone IS. The Greek Septuagint translation of the Hebrew scriptures, and following it the Church's Tradition, understood the divine name in this sense: God is the fullness of Being and of every perfection, without origin and without end. All creatures receive all that they are and have from him; but he alone is his

very being, and he is of himself everything that he is (CCC 213).

God must exist because he is "the ground of existence"; or existence is what he is and every created thing exists only because God sustains it. As St. Paul says of God, "he himself gives to all men life and breath and everything . . . In him we live and move and have our being.'"[2] This makes God, in the words of Pope St. John Paul II, "the supreme Being, the great "Existent."[3] If God is being (not just "a being") who exists without limit, then it follows that God is not limited in his power, knowledge, love, goodness, and ability to exist beyond space and time.

But even if God could be proven to exist, would it be possible to understand such an infinite being? Here we must distinguish between basic understanding and advanced comprehension. I don't *fully comprehend* how every part of a nuclear reactor works, because I'm not a nuclear engineer. But the facts provided by nuclear engineers, which are printed in books, allow me to have a *basic understanding* of how a nuclear reactor works. At a basic level, I understand that we can use nuclear energy to heat water, which creates steam, which spins turbines, which in turn create electricity, although I do not fully comprehend exactly how nuclear reactors work.

Similarly, I may not fully comprehend how God knows all truths or how he created the world, but I can understand that such tasks are not impossible for an infinite being like him. According to the *Catechism*:

> God transcends all creatures. We must therefore continually purify our language of everything in it that is limited, image-bound or imperfect, if we are not to confuse our image of God—"the inexpressible, the incomprehensible, the invisible, the ungraspable"—with our human representations. Our human words always fall short of the mystery of God (CCC 42).

2. What are some false views of God?

Before we explore the attributes and essence of the one true God, let's first examine three common false views of the nature of God.

Polytheism: Monotheists, such as Christians, Muslims, and Jews, believe that only one God exists. Polytheists, on the other hand, believe that many gods exist. The ancient followers of Greek and Roman mythology were examples of polytheists.[4]

Not all ancient Greeks and Romans believed in many gods, however. Philosophers such Plato and Aristotle believed in a supreme being, or God, who created all of reality. In his *Metaphysics*, Aristotle said that gods like Zeus were "myths" but the true God "is a living being, eternal, most good, so that life and duration continuous and eternal belong to God; for this is God."[5]

Unlike the gods of mythological pantheons, the one true God is not confined in any way, not even by space or time. In fact, the orderly behavior of the universe according to fixed, natural laws is evidence for monotheism. If polytheism were true, we would expect the natural order to be disrupted by disagreements or infighting among the gods.[6]

Pantheism: The Pontifical Council for Interreligious Dialogue defined pantheism as the belief that "every element of the universe is divine, and the divinity is equally present in everything. There is no space in this view for God as a distinct being in the sense of classical theism."[7]

According to pantheists, God may be a personal being who comprises the universe or he may be an impersonal force that fills up the universe, but whatever God is, God is not a creator who exists apart from the universe.

As we shall see, however, the universe could have failed to exist, and actually did begin to exist from nothing in the finite past. Therefore, the universe's existence must be explained by a being who is eternal and exists independently of the universe (since it brought the universe into being)—what we know to be the traditional God of monotheism.

A modern variant of pantheism occurs when people reduce God to something in the universe, such as love. Now, it's true that 1 John 4:8 does say, "He who does not love does not know God; for God is love," but as C.S. Lewis said:

Of course, what these people mean when they say that God is love is often something quite different: they really mean "Love is God" . . . [W]hat Christians mean by the statement "God is love" [is that] they believe that the living, dynamic activity of love has been going on in God forever and has created everything else.[8]

Deism: Deists believe that one God created the universe, but, unlike theists, they believe this God no longer interacts with the world he created. Some of the Founding Fathers, such as Thomas Jefferson, were deists. They rejected Christianity, but they did not reject what they called "nature's God." A form of deism that commonly exists among the nonreligious is what some call *moralistic therapeutic deism.*[9] According to this way of thinking, God:

- Exists and watches over the world.

- Wants people to be nice; those nice people go to heaven.

- Is not needed in life unless there is a problem he can solve. This is because the purpose of life is to be happy, not to know and worship God.

The Christian God, though, is not a deistic "absentee landlord," or a shopkeeper who tries to respond to the whims of his human pets. Instead, he is the infinite act of being itself that sustains all of creation. God is just as active in creation now as he was when he brought it into existence in the finite past. According to the *Catechism*, "God does not abandon his creatures to themselves. He not only gives them being and existence, but also, and at every moment, upholds and sustains them in being, enables them to act and brings them to their final end" (CCC 301). In later answers we will see that God revealed himself through Jesus of Nazareth and so, unlike the God of deism, he certainly does care about the eternal fate of his creatures.

3. What are God's key attributes?

In 1215, the Fourth Lateran Council declared that "there is only one true God, eternal and immeasurable, almighty, unchangeable, incomprehensible and ineffable, Father, Son and holy Spirit, three persons but one absolutely simple essence, substance or nature." Let's examine terms like these that are commonly used to describe God.

Simple: God is one, a perfect and infinite act of being. Not even God's attributes are divided; so, for example, God's power is identical to his goodness, which is identical to his knowledge, which is identical to his existence, which is identical to all his other attributes. St. Anselm of Canterbury declared, "[T]here are no parts in you, Lord: neither are you many, but you are so much one and the same with yourself that in nothing are you dissimilar with yourself."[10]

Infinite: When we say that God is infinite, we don't mean that God has an infinite number of thoughts or that he extends over an infinitely long cosmic distance like an infinite series of numbers. Instead, something is infinite if it doesn't have any limits. God is the absolutely simple ground of being itself, and so nothing limits him or his attributes. Instead, God imposes limits on everything else. This understanding of God's infinity helps us further understand God's other attributes.

Necessary: Part of God's infinite nature means there is no limit to his existence. God is therefore *necessary*; that is, he must exist and can never come into existence or go out of existence. God's necessity is unique to him as the Creator. God created all things but nothing created God. Or, as John 1:3 says, "All things were made through him, and without him was not anything made." A first-century text called *The Shepherd of Hermas* shows that the early Church held this view as well. It says, "Believe first of all that God is one, that he created all things and set them in order and brought out of nonexistence into existence everything that is, and that he contains all things while he himself is uncontained."[11]

Immutable: Since God is perfect being, he neither changes nor is changed by anything he creates. As limited beings, we change—for better or for worse. But

God never needs to become better because he is already the best, and he can't change for the worse because all perfections are in his nature. And so he just "is." God is not a being ("the man upstairs") who watches us from heaven and then consciously responds to our choices. This view of God stands in contrast to the false view endorsed by the so-called "process theologians," who say that God only has limited control over his creation and changes in response to it and so "gets better over time" as he governs the creation.[12] As James 1:17 says, God is "the Father of lights with whom there is no variation or shadow due to change."

One: As Deuteronomy 6:4 says, "Hear, O Israel: The Lord our God is one Lord." Since God lacks nothing and is infinite, it follows that there can be only one God. If there were more than one God, then both of those beings would limit each other in some way, thereby negating each being's claim to being infinite. Each of them would lack something the other had, as would be evidenced by our ability to, at least conceptually, distinguish between the two of them.

Eternal and immaterial: God is not limited by either space or time because he created space and time. Tatian the Syrian deftly summarized God's eternality and immaterial nature back in the second century: "Our God has no introduction in time. He alone is without beginning, and is himself the beginning of all things. God is a spirit, not attending upon matter, but the maker of material spirits and of the appearances which are in matter. He is invisible, being himself the Father of both sensible and invisible things."[13]

Omnipresent: God is not "present" everywhere by being identical to everything (as in pantheism) and he is not dispersed through the universe like an invisible gas. Instead of being made up of matter or energy (which would make God an imperfect, pantheistic being), God is present in the universe by sustaining and affecting every part of it according to his divine will.

All-powerful and all-knowing: Omnipotence means God is able to do anything that is logically possible. Omniscience means God knows all real or possibly real things. He knows everything that is as well as everything that could be or could have been. Essentially, God is not limited in either power or knowledge. According to the *Catechism*, "God who created everything also rules everything and can do everything" (CCC 268).

4. Isn't it impossible for a being to be "all-powerful" or "all-knowing?"

Because God sustains all of existence, he must be capable of bringing about any possible state of affairs. The classic argument against God's omnipotence, however, is found in the age-old question: "Can God make a stone so heavy that even he could not lift it?"

If there could be stone he can't lift, then he's not all-powerful. If he couldn't make such a stone, then that's something God can't do, so he is not all-powerful.

However, being omnipotent means that God has the power to do anything *logically possible*. God can do anything that actually can be done, but actions like creating square circles or perfect beings that act imperfectly involve logical contradictions. As a result, they do not fall under the category of "anything that can actually be done." Omnipotence relates to God's ability to actualize the *possible*, so God's omnipotence is not contradicted by his inability to actualize impossible states of affairs. St. Augustine says that God "cannot do some things for the very reason that he is omnipotent."[14] What he means is that God's all-powerful nature would be contradicted if he engaged in acts that made him powerless in some way.

What about God's omniscience, his ability to know all things? Since God sustains all of existence he knows all real and potentially real things. God knows not just everything that is true now, but also every real thing about the past (such as how many steps Alexander the Great took in his lifetime) and every real thing about the future (such as whether you will finish reading this answer).

However, some critics say God can't know everything because he personally doesn't know what it is like to be afraid, even though you and I know what that is like. But omniscience only involves God's knowledge of real or possibly real things. God's inability to know imperfect emotions like fear does not count against his omniscience because God is a perfect being. Certainly, God knows how *I* feel when *I* am afraid but God cannot be afraid because such a condition is impossible for a being who, by definition, can't lack anything.

God is perfect so he cannot suffer pain, loss, or any diminishment. This means God can never be afraid. Since the statement "God is afraid" (and others like it) is meaningless, that is, has no meaning, it can't be true. If it can't be true, it can't be known. And if it can't be known, then it can't contradict God's omniscience, which involves his knowledge of only all real or potentially real things.

Finally, some critics object that if God knows the future then humans can't be free. In their view, if today God knows what I will do tomorrow (like choosing to wear a red shirt), then what I do tomorrow can't change because God's knowledge of the future never changes. I seem destined to wear a certain shirt and do many other things tomorrow because God's foreknowledge cannot be thwarted and can never be incorrect.

Although this kind of puzzle seems troubling at first, we must remember that it does not disprove the existence of God. At best, it may only prove either that humans have no free will or that God doesn't know the future. Of course, Catholics believe that God both knows the future and allows our free choices to be part of his providential plan.

This is possible because God perceives the past, present, and future in one eternal moment. While the future hasn't happened "yet" for you or me, God is aware of it "now," as if it were the present for him. God's knowledge of what I do in the future doesn't *determine* what I do at that time, any more than you observing me wearing a red shirt determines that I wear that particular shirt at that moment. According to the *Catechism*, "To God, all moments of time are present in their immediacy" (CCC 600).

5. How can God be all-good when there is so much evil and suffering in the world?

The problem of evil is one of the oldest and most emotionally powerful arguments for atheism. It's usually formulated in the following way:

1. God must be all-powerful, all-knowing, and all-good.
2. An all-powerful, all-knowing, and all-good being would eliminate evil.
3. Evil exists.
4. Therefore, God does not exist.

Although this argument is emotionally powerful, from a logical perspective it suffers from a glaring weakness. Specifically, it leaves out a key premise that is usually never argued for: "God can have no good reason to allow evil to exist." But St. Thomas Aquinas said that "God allows evils to happen in order to bring a greater good therefrom."[15]

It's important to understand that evil is not created by God. Instead, evil is an absence of good that God tolerates because through it can come a good that he did create. There are two types of evil—moral evil and natural evil. A moral evil occurs when an agent acts against the good, such as a man poisoning his wife so he can marry another woman. Natural evil, on the other hand, occurs when bad effects follow from a morally good or non-moral cause, such as a woman accidentally drinking poison and dying.

Moral evils are privations of the good and represent a defect in the one who is causing the moral evil. God cannot directly create these evils as he has no defects, but he can directly create physical suffering. That's because natural maladies, like pain, can ultimately serve God's good ends and are not inherently evil. Therefore, if God has morally sufficient reason to allow evil or suffering, then what is called the argument from evil for atheism falls apart, because God and the existence of evil are not logically contradictory.

So what reasons might God have for allowing evil to exist?

One reason might be the goal of creating creatures who freely choose the good and avoid evil. If God always compelled human beings to choose the good then our actions would be morally insignificant. They would be no different from the preprogrammed actions of appliances or robots.

But if God allows human beings to choose to love, or to choose the good, then it is possible that some humans may choose evil instead. Thus, some critics might object that if I make a robot that I know will malfunction and hurt other people, then I am responsible for what the robot does. Since God made us and knew we would sin, this makes him responsible for the evil we do. But the problem with this objection is that the robot doesn't *choose* to harm anyone; if it harms someone, it's just following its programming. In that case, we rightly blame the programmer. But human beings aren't robots programmed by God; when they freely choose to do evil we can't blame God for it.

But what about natural evils like disease or disasters? Free will may not explain why God allows these evils, but there may be other reasons why God allows them to exist. First, in a limited, physical world like ours there will always be competing goods that result in natural evils. For example, as fire burns, it consumes the oxygen around it. When a lion eats a zebra and becomes more perfect (becomes healthier, lives longer) it reduces the goodness found in the zebra (the zebra no longer exists).

According to the *Catechism*:

> God freely willed to create a world 'in a state of journeying' towards its ultimate perfection. In God's plan this process of becoming involves the appearance of certain beings and the disappearance of others, the existence of the more perfect alongside the less perfect, both constructive and destructive forces of nature. With physical good there exists also *physical evil* as long as creation has not reached perfection (CCC 310).

Second, natural evils may serve to build our character and help us develop virtue that could not exist in a world that is immediately brought to perfection. For example, it's impossible for God to make someone be courageous if he is not in danger. Likewise, it is impossible for God to make someone be compassionate if that person cannot empathize with or sacrifice for a person who is suffering. Therefore, these goods could not exist without certain kinds of suffering that accompany them. Third, as limited human beings we are simply not in a good position to know the good that God can bring hundreds or even thousands of years later from the evil and suffering we face in the present.

It's interesting to ponder how atheists define evil. They know it can't be defined solely as pain or suffering, because sometimes pain or suffering can be a good thing (such a criminal's punishment or an athlete's enduring hardship while training). Instead, evil can best be described as "unwarranted suffering" or "a state of affairs that is not supposed to be." But this implies that there is "a way things are supposed to be"—a notion that doesn't make sense in an accidental, atheistic universe, but does make sense in a universe created by God.

When we review the evidence for God's existence (which we'll do later), we see that it outweighs the doubts caused by evil and suffering. As a result, we can know that God exists and that he will bring a greater good from evil, even if we don't know in the present moment what that good might be.

6. Hasn't science made God unnecessary?

An argument called "God of the gaps" claims that a currently unexplained phenomenon of the natural world is proof that God exists, because only God's existence can explain it. For example, ancient people who did not know what caused lightning might have assumed that a god caused it to punish mankind. Of course, this kind of argument for the existence of God ignores the fact that a suitable natural explanation for the unknown phenomenon may eventually be discovered, and we will miss it if we rush to the conclusion that "God did it!" This happened, for example, when

Isaac Newton said that the best explanation for the motion of the planets was that an intelligent agent or even angels were pushing them.

We must also be wary of similar arguments that claim that certain features of the human cell, or certain organs, could not have arisen by natural means, so therefore a supernatural explanation is required. But if a natural explanation were later found for what we can't explain, then our evidence for God will have disappeared as the gap in our understanding is closed by scientific discovery. Science can't prove God exists simply by pointing to natural phenomena that human beings cannot yet explain. It also can't disprove God's existence, because science cannot make judgments about entities that exist beyond the natural world.

So how does science relate to God? St. Thomas Aquinas provides us with a model of the traditional relationship between science and natural theology, that is, coming to know God through reason. Thomas used scientific facts such as the presence of change or the regularity of movement within natural bodies as premises in *philosophical* arguments for the existence of God. So for example, Thomas showed that the motion we empirically observe in the world could be logically traced back to an unmoved mover or God. The *Catechism* states that scientific discoveries should "invite us to even greater admiration for the greatness of the Creator" (CCC 283).

The very idea that science should be the primary way we learn about the world comes from a modern conception of science. During the Middle Ages, science was defined as "the knowledge of things from their causes."[16] Using this definition, even theology was considered a science because it involved a quest for knowledge (the Latin word for which is *scientia*). But after the work of modern thinkers such as Isaac Newton and Galileo Galilei, the concept of "science" shrank to accommodate what had once been called natural philosophy or natural science. In 1837, William Whewell coined the term *scientist* to describe a person who seeks systematic explanations for observed phenomena.

Science is a helpful tool when it comes to understanding the world, but it's not the *only* tool we use to understand the world, any more than a hammer is the only tool we use to build a house. The danger we face today is that both professional scientists and a growing number of laypeople rely on science to be the sole arbiter of truth. Physicists Stephen Hawking and Leonard Mlodinow wrote in their book *The Grand Design*, "What is the nature of reality? Where did all this come from? Did the universe need a creator? . . . Traditionally these are questions for philosophy, but philosophy is dead. Philosophy has not kept up with modern developments in science, particularly physics. Scientists have become the bearers of the torch of discovery in our quest for knowledge."[17]

But the torch of science can't illuminate the answer to every question we have about the world. For example, science relies on philosophy in order to know what science even is, how science works, and what counts as science. It is philosophy that helps distinguish the legitimate sciences of astronomy and chemistry from the pseudo-sciences of astrology and alchemy.

Science also relies on the philosophical assumption that the world operates under scientific laws that are not only the same across the universe but also the same yesterday and tomorrow. There is no experiment that can validate these philosophical assumptions; they must instead be "taken on faith." Moreover, since modern science is restricted to the search for natural explanations that can be tested, it must be neutral on the question of whether God exists. Science cannot disprove God, nor can it invoke God as part of a scientific theory, because God's existence can't be tested.

Science is an excellent tool for learning about the natural world, but it is not a magic bullet that can remedy or explain everything, nor was it ever meant to carry such a burden.

7. Does the universe provide evidence that God exists?

The famous contemporary philosopher Derek Parfit wrote: "Why is there a universe at all? It might have been true that nothing ever existed: no living beings, no stars, no atoms, not even space or time. When we think about this, it can seem astonishing that anything exists."[18]

To be *contingent* means that something doesn't have to exist; it could be different, or it could not *be* at all. Contingent things need other things in order to stay in existence. For example, humans need the oxygen plants create, the oxygen we breathe needs an atmosphere, the atmosphere requires the planet's gravity in order to stay together, and so on. We know that humans are contingent because we can imagine a world without them. We can do the same for other contingent objects, such as stars and planets. We can even agree with Derek Parfit that the universe as a whole is contingent and so there must be some reason that explains why it exists.

Something is *necessary,* on the other hand, when it is not contingent and so could not be different or could not *not be.* The three sides of a triangle are necessary to a triangle because it is impossible to draw a triangle with more or fewer sides. This fact can't be different, so we can say that three sides are necessary to a triangle. In the same way, God's existence is necessary because God cannot "not exist." The contingency argument for the existence of God claims that the universe's existence seems to be dependent on something that is not dependent upon anything else. A contingent universe like ours depends on a "necessary" being like God in order to exist.

There are a few ways an atheist could respond to an argument like this. One would be to deny that an explanation for the existence of the universe is needed. But the philosopher Richard Taylor offers an excellent illustration of why it is a mistake to say the universe does not need an explanation for its existence.[19] He asks us to imagine walking through the woods with a friend and coming across a glowing ball on the ground. If we saw something like that, we would certainly want to know where it came from. We would be unsatisfied if our friend said, "The ball is just there, and that's all." Even if it turned out the ball was eternal and had always existed, we would want to know why such an amazing object existed at all.

Now, what if the ball were the size of a car? Or a blimp? Or a planet? Wouldn't we still wonder what its explanation is? What if the ball were the size of the whole universe? Changing the object's size does nothing to remove the need to explain its existence.

Another way an atheist could respond to the contingency argument would be to say that the universe has to exist—that it is necessary, and thus explains itself. But consider the question "Why does this universe exist?" Does it more closely resemble the question "Why is that triangle red?" or "Why does that triangle have three sides?" We can imagine triangles that aren't red, but can't envision a triangle that has more or fewer than three sides. Since we can imagine nothing existing at all, the question of why the universe exists seems to be more like the "what color" question than the "number of sides" question. Since the color of a triangle is explained by something outside of the triangle, and the universe's existence is as contingent as a triangle's color—meaning that it could just as easily not have existed—it follows that the reason the universe exists must be found in something outside of the universe.

A third response would be to ask why God is the explanation for the universe's existence. Why can't the explanation be another universe? What is God's explanation for why he exists? But asking what explains the existence of God is like asking what causes triangles to have three sides or fire to be hot. The answer is explained in the definition of the thing itself. Fire's nature is to be hot, a triangle's nature is to be three-sided, and God's nature is to exist because he is existence itself.

The same can't be said of other contingent realities. For example, the argument that a parallel universe caused our universe would be no explanation for why our universe exists. It would be like saying a boxcar on a train moves because it is pulled by the boxcar in front of it, which in turn is pulled by the boxcar in front of it, and so on. But one or a million boxcars depend on something else in order to move; they cannot move themselves. Therefore, even an infinite number of boxcars could not move a single inch. They must be moved by something that moves itself, such as a locomotive.

Likewise, a large or even infinite series of universes or physical forces didn't have to exist and thus cannot explain their own existence. These things would still need to be explained by a cause that cannot fail to exist, a necessary cause that sustains not only the whole collection of contingent universes but the matter and forces that exist within those universes as well. Because it is necessary, this cause also couldn't be created or destroyed—in other words, it would be what you and I call God.

8. Does the Big Bang provide evidence for the existence of God?

In the early twentieth century, the Belgian priest and physicist Fr. Georges Lemaître concluded that Einstein's new theory of gravity, called general relativity, would cause a static eternal universe to collapse into nothingness. Since Einstein's theory was sound, this meant only one thing: the universe was not static but growing, and had a beginning in the finite past. Fr. Lemaître and Einstein even discussed the cosmic consequences of the theory while walking around the campus of Caltech. Although Einstein was skeptical at first, in 1933 he proclaimed that Fr. Lemaître's theory of an expanding universe was one of the most "beautiful theories he had ever heard."[20]

Fr. Lemaître called his theory "the primeval atom," but another physicist, Fred Hoyle, mocked it with the term "Big Bang." Hoyle wanted to discredit the theory as nothing more than religious propaganda, but the movement of stars away from each other and the cosmic radiation that permeated the whole galaxy provided almost indisputable evidence that the Big Bang did happen—evidence not for an *explosion in space*, but an *expansion of space* (as well as time, matter, and energy) from an infinitely dense point, called a singularity.[21] According to renowned Tufts University cosmologist Alexander Vilenkin, "All the evidence we have says that the universe had a beginning."[22]

Now, we should remember that all appeals to scientific evidence for the beginning of the universe can never be 100 percent certain. We should be open to where the evidence leads but we should also be aware of the history of cosmology, and how multiple, independent lines of evidence have been added to confirm the standard Big Bang model over the past century. The distinguished British astronomer Martin Rees wrote: "Cosmological ideas are no longer any more fragile and evanescent than our theories about the history of our earth . . . The empirical support for a Big Bang ten to fifteen billion years ago is as compelling as the evidence that geologists offer on our earth's history."[23]

So if the universe began to exist, what can we conclude? One intuition most people have is summarized in the Latin phrase *ex nihilo, nihil fit*, or "Out of nothing, nothing comes."[24] It makes sense that "nothing" (not just black or empty space, but "no thing") is incapable of doing anything. As the philosopher John Locke put it, "Man knows, by an intuitive certainty, that bare nothing can no more produce any real being, than it can be equal to two right angles."[25]

Some atheists say that even if the universe began to exist at the Big Bang, it could have emerged from a state of nothingness similar to the way virtual particles have been observed in physics laboratories to come to be from nothing. Or the universe could have come from an infinite number of other universes stretching backward in time before the Big Bang. However, both of these explanations are problematic.

First, virtual particles do not pop into existence from pure nothingness. Instead, they come from a quantum vacuum, or a low-level energy field that can fluctuate. As philosopher and theoretical physicist David Albert writes:

Vacuum states—no less than giraffes or refrigerators or solar systems—are particular arrangements of *elementary physical stuff* . . . The fact that particles can pop in and out of existence, over time, as those [quantum] fields rearrange themselves, is not a whit more mysterious than the fact that fists can pop in and out of existence, over time, as my fingers rearrange themselves. And none of these poppings—if you look at them aright—amount to anything even remotely in the neighborhood of a creation from nothing.[26]

Other physicists have shown that an infinite series of collapsing and expanding universes could not have caused the universe we observe today because the amount of disorder we observe in our universe is far lower than it would be if the past were eternal.[27] A better explanation for the data we observe is that the universe, which includes all of space, time, matter, and energy, began to exist and that it came into existence from an "uncaused cause" that transcends space and time, or what we call God.

9. Did God create the world?

Some atheists think they can refute the previous first-cause arguments for God by asking the simple question, "If everything needs a cause, then what caused God?" But everything does not need a cause. Instead, only those things that began to exist or don't have to exist require a cause. Since the universe did not have to exist and there is good evidence that it began to exist, then it requires an explanation for why it exists. God, on the other hand, never began to exist because he is eternal (he created time itself). Therefore, God requires no cause for his existence, but the universe coming to be from nothing does require an "uncaused cause," or God, to explain why it exists.

But why not think that the cause of the universe is an alien from another universe, or maybe some kind of impersonal force? First, since the cause of the universe was responsible for the existence of space and time, it must also be immune to the restrictions of space and time (that is, be immaterial and eternal). This means the first cause could not be a material object (like an alien). Also, the forces we are aware of, like gravity, exist within the space-time universe, so they could not be responsible for the creation of space and time.

Second, the cause of the universe could not be some impersonal force because prior to the creation of the universe there was only a time-less, space-less, unchangeable state of affairs (remember, time and space came into existence at the Big Bang).[28] An eternal, impersonal force would blindly generate an effect for all eternity. But since the universe is not eternal, it follows that a personal being chose to create a finite universe and the universe was not the product of an eternal, impersonal force.

The Fourth Lateran Council declared that God is the "creator of all things invisible and visible, spiritual and corporeal; who by his almighty power at the beginning of time created from nothing."[29] The *Catechism* also affirms that "God needs no pre-existent thing or any help in order to create, nor is creation any sort of necessary emanation from the divine substance. God creates freely 'out of nothing'" (CCC 296). This doctrine is called *creatio ex nihilo*, or "creation from nothing," and can be known from reason: if God created the universe, and the universe is finite, then God could not have rearranged eternally preexisting matter in order to make the universe. He must instead have brought the universe into being from nothing through an act of his will.

The Bible and the Church Fathers also testify to this doctrine. The psalmist tells the stars to "praise the name of the Lord! For he commanded and they were created" and the mother in 2 Maccabees told her sons, "look at the heaven and the earth and see everything that is in them, and recognize that God did not make them out of things that existed" (2 Macc. 7:28). Hebrews 11:3 says that "the world was created by the word of God, so that what is seen was made out of things which do not appear" (or, in other translations, "was not made out of visible things"). The first-century author of *The Shepherd of Hermas* declares that God "created all things and set them in order and brought out of nonexistence into existence everything that is."[30]

Other critics object that if God is perfect then why did he create the universe? Wouldn't God only have created the universe because he lacked something, and if he lacked something, then wouldn't that mean he was not perfect? However, there's no need to presume that God would only have created the universe to fill some void in his life, or out of loneliness or boredom. Since God is the perfection of virtues, including love and selflessness, then his creation of the universe is the logical result of his superabundant love and self-giving. God created the universe not for his good, but for ours (CCC 293).

St. Theophilus of Antioch wrote in the second century, "God made all things out of nothing; for nothing was co-eternal with God: but he being his own place, and wanting nothing, and existing before the ages, willed to make man by whom he might be known; *for him* [man], therefore, he prepared the world."[31]

10. Doesn't evolution disprove the existence of God?

There is no conflict in believing in the existence of God and believing in the biological theory of evolution. In fact, in a 2007 address, Pope Benedict XVI said,

> There are so many scientific proofs in favor of evolution, which appears to be a reality we can see and which enriches our knowledge of life and being as such. But . . . the doctrine of evolution does not answer every query, especially the great philosophical question: Where does everything come from? And how did everything start which ultimately led to man? I believe this is of the utmost importance.[32]

The Catholic Church teaches that the first eleven chapters of Genesis contain historical truths that answer these basic questions, affirming that God created everything and made humans in his image in order for them to know and adore him. But those chapters, in the words of Pope Pius XII, "state the principal truths which are fundamental for our salvation, and also give a popular description of the origin of the human race and the chosen people."[33] They do not assert in scientific terms the origins of the earth and its inhabitants. The Catholic Church has infallibly taught that God created the world from nothing by his own will and that he made man's immortal soul in his own image.[34] The Church has not, however, taught how God created the world or how old creation is. A Catholic is free to form his own opinions on those questions.

But evolution, far from disproving the existence of God, forces us to ask the question, "Why do we live in a universe where the evolution of life is even possible?" In the past fifty years, scientists have discovered that there is a wide variety of constants and conditions that could have made up the laws of nature. Even a slight variation in many of these finely tuned laws would have spelled disaster for life as we know it.

For example, gravity is 10^{36} times weaker than competing forces within atoms, a critical fact for all living things.[35] As a 2009 article in *New Scientist* magazine put it:

The feebleness of gravity is something we should be grateful for. If it were a tiny bit stronger, none of us would be here to scoff at its puny nature . . . Only the middle ground, where the expansion and the gravitational strength balance to within one part in 10^{15} [a quadrillion] at one second after the Big Bang, allows life to form.[36]

Another example is the cosmological constant, which represents the strength of gravity in an empty vacuum of space and controls how fast the universe expands. Once thought to be zero, this constant is actually fine-tuned to the 120th power—a decimal point with 119 zeros and a one. In other words, the constant could have been 10^{120} times larger than a life-permitting value; what is the explanation for this incredibly small, yet nonzero value? Alexander Vilenkin wrote: "A tiny deviation from the required power results in a cosmological disaster, such as the fireball collapsing under its own weight or the universe being nearly empty. . . . This is the most notorious and perplexing case of fine-tuning in physics."[37]

String theorist Leonard Susskind, like Vilenkin a nonreligious scientist, writes in his article, "Disturbing Implications of the Cosmological Constant," that unless this constant was fine-tuned, "statistically miraculous events" would be needed for our universe to be life-permitting. He suggests that, in light of this, it is possible that an unknown agent set the early conditions of the universe we observe today.[38]

Now, some people will say that the universe is not "fine-tuned" for life because so much of it is hostile to life (such as the vacuum of space), but this misunderstands the fine-tuning argument. To say the universe is fine-tuned for life does not mean it is a place where the maximum amount of life will thrive. Fine-tuning only means that out of all the possible universes that could exist, it is much more likely that there would have been no life at all. The fact that our universe does accommodate life against such incredible odds requires an explanation, regardless of how much, or how little, life it accommodates.

So what explains this fine-tuning? There's no reason to think the laws of nature *must* be life-permitting, since we can imagine them being different. Pure chance also seems to be an extremely unlikely explanation, because the odds of getting all the constants and conditions right are on par with winning fifty consecutive hands of poker with royal flushes every time! (Or one in 10^{300}, and that's a conservative estimate)[39] If we reject chance as an explanation for such an improbable poker game, shouldn't we reject chance to explain an even more improbable universe?

Another possibility is that our universe is the one lucky universe that happens to support life, amid an infinite sea of dead universes contained within a larger "multiverse." However, there is little non-speculative evidence for the multiverse, and many scientists treat it as almost a religious hypothesis. Rather than solve the problem of fine-tuning, it pushes the problem one step further back. The non-Christian physicist Paul Davies summarizes the futility of explaining fine-tuning with the multiverse hypothesis:

> So is that the end of the story? Can the multiverse provide a complete and closed account of all physical existence? Not quite. The multiverse comes with a lot of baggage, such as an overarching space and time to host all those bangs, a universe-generating mechanism to trigger them, physical fields to populate the universes with material stuff, and a selection of forces to make things happen. Cosmologists embrace these features by envisaging sweeping "meta-laws" that pervade the multiverse and spawn specific bylaws on a universe-by-universe basis. The meta-laws themselves remain unexplained—eternal, immutable transcendent entities that just happen to exist and must simply be accepted as given. In that respect the meta-laws have a similar status to an unexplained transcendent god.[40]

11. Do I need to believe in God in order to be a good person?

There are many moral nonbelievers, and some of them even surpass Christians in their moral behavior. So, no, belief in God is not necessary in order to be a good person. But God must exist in order for the concept of a "good person" to be coherent, or for morals in general to be objective (for example, why the statement "It is always wrong to torture children for fun" is always true). Of course, many atheists say morality can be grounded in other things besides God, but these proposals have serious flaws.

For example, some atheists ground moral truths in our biology. They suggest that as our species evolved, human beings who acted in moral ways (for example, by cooperating with other humans rather than killing or stealing from them) lived longer than those who didn't. After millions of years, we developed an instinct to be moral. Of course, even if evolution could explain *why* we act in certain ways, it doesn't explain why we *should* or *should not* act in those ways.

If morals only exist to help us survive and pass on our genes, then they are not commandments we are bound to obey but merely helpful suggestions that can assist the survival of our "herd." If our community decided, for example, to kill handicapped children after birth in order to weed out genetic abnormalities and improve herd health, it would be moral. But our moral intuition tells us that killing children is wrong, regardless of how it might help our species, so it follows that morality doesn't come from evolution.

Another proposed way to ground morality apart from God would be to say that the consensus of a community decides what is moral or immoral. But if this were so, then we couldn't say that any other society is more or less moral, only that they are all different. We couldn't say that a society that agreed to permit child-killing was any less moral than a society that prohibited it. Even worse, what would we make of efforts to reform society? Martin Luther King Jr. thought racist laws in American society were wrong and had to change, and many atheists would agree with him. But if morality comes from society, then society—even when it makes racist laws—can *never* be immoral.

But couldn't morality just be like the law of gravity, just something that exists in nature and transcends humans but is unrelated to God? No, because moral truths aren't *descriptive* truths—like the law of gravity—which merely say what will happen. They are instead what philosophers call *prescriptive* truths, or truths that say what *should* happen or what moral beings should do in a given circumstance. The law of gravity says that, all things being equal, an object pushed over a cliff will fall and hit the ground below. But the law of morality says that one *should not* push grandma over the cliff in order to kill her. Since laws of nature cannot be disobeyed (if you jump off a cliff, gravity will take over no matter what you think of it), and moral laws can be disobeyed, it follows that morality is not a mere law of nature.

Some people will say, however, that morality can't be grounded in God because if God commanded us to do something evil, like torture a child, it wouldn't become moral just because God commanded it. Therefore, something over and above God must exist in order to ground morality and determine these acts are objectively evil.

But because God is a perfect and infinite being who exists without limit or flaw he will necessarily command only good acts that correspond with his perfect nature. God could never will us to do anything evil, because he is goodness itself and desires that we be made holy because he is holy (1 Pet. 1:16). The *Catechism*, quoting St. Thomas Aquinas, teaches that "God's almighty power is in no way arbitrary: 'In God, power, essence, will, intellect, wisdom, and justice are all identical. Nothing therefore can be in God's power which could not be in his just will or his wise intellect'" (CCC 271).

So, in conclusion, one can be a good person without believing in God, but without God goodness itself loses its meaning.

12. Does God have a body? Is God a "he"?

Even though the Catholic Church teaches that God is immaterial and transcends the universe, some religions, such as Mormonism, teach that God is a material being like you or me and has a physical body. Defenders of this view quote Genesis 1:26, which records God saying, "Let us make man in our image, after our likeness." If we are made in God's image, then shouldn't our bodies look like God's body?

Other critics defend the idea that God has a physical body by pointing to Scripture passages that describe God sitting on a throne (Psalm 47:8), having a right hand (Acts 7:55–56), and appearing to human beings in bodily form. One example of this would be Moses seeing God's "back" (Exod. 33:23) and speaking with God "face to face, as a man speaks to his friend" (Exod. 33:11). But we must be careful when we interpret verses that use non-literal language to communicate a spiritual truth about God. For example, Psalm 91:4 says God "will cover you with his pinions [feathers], and under his wings you will find refuge," but this passage teaches us about God's love for us, not his wingspan.

The biblical descriptions of God having a human body are not literal because reason shows us that God is the immaterial creator of the universe and Scripture teaches us that God is invisible (Col. 1:15, 1 Tim. 1:17). 1 Timothy 6:16 says that God "dwells in unapproachable light, whom no man has ever seen or can see." When Exodus tells us Moses spoke to God "face to face," it was an expression of the intimacy Moses had with God. God himself told Moses, "you cannot see my face; for man shall not see me and live" (Exod. 33:20). In addition, being "made in the image of God" means humans have rational abilities and resemble

God in an immaterial way, such as by being loving or just (CCC 357). It does not mean God has a physical body like ours.

In fact, John 4:24 says, "God is spirit," and Jesus makes it clear in Luke 24:39 that "a spirit has not flesh and bones." The idea that God is a spirit and not a man was also the common understanding of God in the early Church. The second-century Church Father St. Irenaeus taught that God "is simple, not composed of parts, without structure, altogether like and equal to himself alone. He is all mind, all spirit."[41] It's important to remember that although God is a spirit he is also all-powerful. He can do anything that is logically possible, including becoming man (such as when God the Son became the man Jesus Christ). Although God can acquire a human body if he wants one, God doesn't *need* a body (God the Father and God the Son exist without one).

But if God doesn't have a body and isn't a man in his divine nature, then in what sense can God be called a "he"?

It has become fashionable in some circles to refer to God as "she" or to avoid gender pronouns entirely when referring to God. However, the *Catechism* explains:

By calling God "Father," the language of faith indicates two main things: that God is the first origin of everything and transcendent authority; and that he is at the same time goodness and loving care for all his children. God's parental tenderness can also be expressed by the image of motherhood, which emphasizes God's immanence, the intimacy between Creator and creature . . . God transcends the human distinction between the sexes. He is neither man nor woman: he is God. He also transcends human fatherhood and motherhood, although he is their origin and standard: no one is father as God is Father (CCC 239).

The philosophers Peter Kreeft and Ronald Tacelli give us another reason to explain why God revealed himself as "he" instead of as "she" or "it." They say the Jewish religion was distinct in exclusively using male pronouns for the divine because this underscores how God is the distinct, transcendent creator of the universe. They write, "As a man comes into a woman from without to make her pregnant, so God creates the universe from without rather than birthing it from within."[42]

13. Is the God of theistic philosophers the same as the God of the Bible?

As we've already seen, when the Bible describes God having a body or being a "he," it is using metaphors to explain eternal truths about God to finite human beings—us. But its use of such metaphors doesn't mean that the biblical God is different from the infinite, necessary, simple, and flawless being posited by philosophers.

Some atheists object that the God of the Bible seems emotionally dysfunctional because the Bible says he is "wrathful" toward sinners and "jealous" when they worship other gods. But we need not take these descriptions to mean that the biblical God has emotions in the sense that we do—immediate, affective responses to stimuli. Nothing can change or surprise the all-knowing God. He doesn't exhibit the emotions we do when we react to new situations. So when the Bible describes God having emotions like anger, regret, or pleasure, it is using metaphors to describe how human beings relate to God—not the other way around. Catholic philosopher Patrick Lee writes that God can be said to be pleased or angry with us "in the relational sense"; that is, "we are related to God as one who pleases is related to the one who is pleased . . . We are related to God as one who elicits anger is related to the one who is angry."[43]

In other words, saying that God is angry at our sin, or pleased with our obedience, doesn't describe God reacting to something we have done. Instead, it is a non-literal way of describing the consequences our own actions have in regards to our relationship with God. Positive actions draw us closer to God whereas negative actions push us away from him. Saying that

God is jealous of other gods means that God does not will that we worship false gods, who are morally and metaphysically inferior to the one true God.

Other passages in Scripture that ascribe emotions to God must also be understood in this non-literal, relational sense. For example, the last verse of the book of Jonah says, "When God saw what they did, how they turned from their evil way, God repented of the evil which he had said he would do to them; and he did not do it" (Jon. 3:10). But how can an immutable God change his mind? Wouldn't an omniscient being know about his future change of mind before it occurred? The phrase "God repented" tells us that God would no longer execute his judgment upon the people of Nineveh. When the Bible says that God changed or repented from evil, it is a metaphorical way of saying that human beings have changed, or that human beings have repented, not that God has changed in any way. God knew the people of Nineveh would eventually repent, but he sent Jonah to them because *the people of Nineveh* did not know they were capable of such repentance.

When we encounter Biblical descriptions of God that seem "too human," we must remember a principle of revelation called *divine condescension*. This is the act by which God stoops down to our level so that we finite humans can better understand him. For example, God must assume some kind of visual or auditory form to relate to humans, even though he is not composed of matter. Or, God must speak to humans in sentences even though his knowledge exists as a perfect, timeless whole and he does not "think" about anything.

St. John Chrysostom said that even the angels who surrounded God's throne in Isaiah 6:1–2 did not see God's true glory. He writes, "Yet they did not see the pure light itself nor the pure essence itself. What they saw was a condescension accommodated to their nature. What is this condescension? God condescends whenever he is not seen as he is, but in the way one incapable of beholding him is able to look upon him. In this way God reveals himself by accommodating what he reveals to the weakness of vision of those who behold him."[44]

14. Can human beings become gods?

The Church of Jesus Christ of Latter-day Saints (also known as the Mormon or LDS Church) teaches that it is possible for human beings to become gods. Their founder, Joseph Smith, said, "God himself was once as we are now, and is an exalted man, and sits enthroned in yonder heavens!"[45] The fifth president of the LDS Church, Lorenzo Snow, summarized this teaching in the famous couplet:

As man now is, God once was;
As God now is, man may be.

The idea that human beings can become gods is also common in New Age religions and can be traced as far back as the Devil's temptation of Adam and Eve. He said, "When you eat of [the forbidden fruit] your eyes will be opened, and you will be like God" (Gen. 3:5).

However, there can be only one God, because God is the infinite, undivided being—he is not just one "super being" among other beings. In Isaiah 44:8 God says, "Is there a God besides me? . . . I know not any." If the God of this world were omniscient, then wouldn't he know about the other God he worshipped when he was a man? God also makes it clear in Isaiah 43:10 that before him "no god was formed, nor shall there be any after me." This can't refer to false gods or idols, because many of those are still "formed" to this day. Instead, the Bible teaches us that no other God besides the one true God has ever existed and no other God will ever exist.

Scripture emphatically teaches that there is only one God and that we are to worship him alone. Deuteronomy 4:39 says, "Know therefore this day, and lay it to your heart, that the Lord is God in heaven above and on the earth beneath; there is no other." In Isaiah 45:5 God says, "I am the Lord, and there is no other, besides me there is no God." Jesus described God as "the only God" (John 5:44) and "the only true God" (John 17:3). St. Paul describes God as "the only wise God" (Rom. 16:27) and the only being who possesses immortality (1 Tim. 6:16). St. Ignatius of Antioch wrote in the early second century that the early Christians were persecuted because they "convince[d] the unbelieving . . . that there is one God, who has manifested himself by Jesus Christ his Son."[46]

God is, by definition, an eternal and unchanging being, so the God we worship could not have previously been a man (as Mormons believe). Malachi 3:6 says, "I the Lord do not change," and Psalm 90:2 says, "from everlasting to everlasting thou art God." From one infinite direction to another infinite direction, God is literally always God and is never anything else. God could never at any time have been "not God," and he could never have been an imperfect, mortal human being. Numbers 23:19 says, "God is not man, that he should lie, or a son of man, that he should repent," and in Hosea 11:9 God emphatically declares, "I am God and not man."

Some critics who believe that men can become gods cite paragraph 460 of the *Catechism*, which quotes Sts. Athanasius and Thomas Aquinas, "The Word became flesh to make us 'partakers of the divine nature': 'For the Son of God became man so that we might become God. The only-begotten Son of God, wanting to make us sharers in his divinity, assumed our nature, so that he, made man, might make men gods.'"

Now, the Catholic Church does teach that humans can, through the grace of God, acquire God's shareable (or communicable) attributes such as holiness or impartiality. This is what Athanasius meant when he said, "we might become God." But Athanasius also said that "we become by grace what God is by nature." That is, God gives us the gift of sharing his divine life so that we *resemble* him, but we never *become* him.[47]

Renowned historian of Christianity Jaroslav Pelikan says that the doctrine that men could become like God in holiness (what is called *divinization* or *theosis*) was, among people like Athanasius, "not to be viewed as analogous to Classical Greek theories about the promotion of human beings to divine rank, and in that sense not to be defined by natural theology at all; on such errors they pronounced their 'Anathema!'"[48] The Church Fathers who spoke of *theosis,* then, would not have recognized the Mormon doctrine of exaltation as a variation of it. They would have considered it a grave heresy.

15. Does God perform miracles?

As we saw earlier, the biggest difference between the God of deism and the God of classical theism is that the former does not interact with the world he created. Deists often say that for God to do so—through the extraordinary interventions we call miracles—would require breaking the perfect laws of nature he created.

But the laws of nature are not like traffic laws, to be obeyed or to be broken. Instead, the laws of nature (such as gravity) merely describe how events usually occur. Since God has complete control over all of reality, he can intervene in the natural order and cause things to happen that are out of the ordinary (such as a man walking on the surface of liquid water). This does not violate the laws of nature because these laws only describe what *usually* happens in a certain physical system. They do not mandate what must always take place in those systems.

According to the *Catechism*, "God willed that external proofs of his Revelation [such as Christian miracles or the holiness of the Church] should be joined to the internal helps of the Holy Spirit . . . they are 'motives of credibility' (*motiva credibilitatis*), which show that the assent of faith is 'by no means a blind impulse of the mind'" (CCC 156). In other words, God allows the world to naturally progress on its own but does intervene on occasion. Those interventions (for example, miracles) provide reasons for the faith we have in God and his revelation to us.

But why do we only believe in the miracles of the God of Christianity? Why don't we believe in the miracle-stories of other religions, like Buddhism or Islam? One reason is that there is a difference in the quality of the evidence for Christ's miracles and those of other faiths. For example, our earliest report of Jesus' Resurrection comes from St. Paul, a former skeptic who knew the original apostles. He testifies to the nearly immediate belief the apostles and first Christians had in Jesus' Resurrection; it was not the fruit of later legend.

This differs sharply from the miracles associated with Buddha and Muhammad, which were recorded hundreds of years after they were dead. Those miracles appear to be "legendary layers" added on to the lives of persuasive yet mortal preachers who both refused to perform miracles in their own lifetimes—in contrast to Jesus, for whom miracles were an essential part of his ministry.[49]

Christ's Resurrection from the dead vindicated his divine claims, and all natural explanations for the Resurrection accounts fail to make sense of the evidence. For example, it won't do to say that the accounts are legendary since we have the letters of Paul, and he personally knew Peter and the other apostles who witnessed and preached the Resurrection (Gal. 1:18–19, 1 Cor. 15:3–7). There must instead be some explanation for why they preached that their dead rabbi had come back to life.

It would not suffice to say that they lied about it for material gain or fame, as those apostles were persecuted and martyred for their faith, and not one ever recanted. It also wouldn't work to say the apostles hallucinated the Resurrection, because they saw Jesus in groups on some occasions (1 Cor. 15:5–7), and it is almost always individuals, not groups, who experience hallucinations.

A further problem with this theory is that a physical resurrection from the dead is most likely not what the apostles would have imagined. Historian N.T. Wright, in his book *The Resurrection of the Son of God,* scoured the ancient literature and found no examples in the pagan world or in Jewish thought of the belief in a person dying, experiencing the afterlife, and then returning to a glorified, immortal, bodily existence in the present life. If the apostles had somehow all hallucinated, or projected something that would have been plausible and familiar to them, most likely they would have imagined something in line with established belief, such as a Christ who had been spiritually assumed into heaven. The apostles, however, emphatically did not preach this, but rather that Jesus had been raised bodily from the dead.[50]

Even if the apostles could have found motivation to believe in Jesus without the Resurrection, no such motivation existed for Jesus' enemies. Saul of Tarsus (later Paul the apostle) was a Pharisee who persecuted the ancient Church; James, likely one of Jesus' relatives, may have initially rejected him.[51] But after an encounter with the risen Christ, Saul completely reversed his beliefs and joined the Jewish heresy he had been persecuting; James would be martyred for his belief in Christ. What else besides an actual encounter with the risen Christ can explain their sudden and startling conversions?

16. What is the Trinity?

Put simply, the Christian doctrine of the Trinity states that God is one being who exists as three divine persons—the Father, Son, and Holy Spirit. According to the *Catechism*, "We do not confess three Gods, but one God in three persons, the 'consubstantial Trinity.' The divine persons do not share the one divinity among themselves but each of them is God whole and entire" (CCC 253). The *Catechism* also teaches that the Trinity does not contradict God's simplicity because each person fully dwells in one another and they are distinguished relationally, not spatially or temporally into different "parts" of God.[52]

In order to understand the doctrine, we must first understand three key words: being, person, and nature. A *being* is a unified entity; a *person* is "who someone is"; and a *nature* refers to "what something is" or to what kind a being belongs. For example, you are a kind of being (in this case, an animal) as well as a person. You also have a human nature, that is, you have the capacity to act in distinctly human ways. So you are a *being* who is one *person* who possesses one human *nature*.

So how does this relate to God? Christians do not believe that God is *one person* with infinite attributes. That belief, held for example by Jews and Muslims, is called unitarianism. Christians instead believe that God is *one being* who exists as *three persons*, each of whom fully possess the divine *nature*. Christians are not unitarians but trinitarians. They believe that, because there is only one God, and the Father is God, the Son is God, and the Holy Spirit is God, it follows that this one God must exist as three coequal and coeternal persons. Matthew 28:19 hints at this reality when it says that Jesus commanded baptism in the *name* (not names) of the Father, and of Son, and of the Holy Spirit.

The Trinity can't be grasped if we think of "beings" and "persons" as the same thing. But if we recognize that there are beings that are zero persons (such as rocks and trees) and there are beings that are one person (humans and angels), then we see that there could be a being that is three persons.

It's also important to avoid confusing analogies that misrepresent the Trinity. For example, saying the Trinity is like a clover that is one leaf with three petals endorses the heresy of tritheism, or the belief that the Father, Son, and Holy Spirit are individual beings who share a part of the divine nature, not three persons united in one Godhead. Another faulty analogy is saying that the Trinity is like one man being a father, husband, and son at the same time. This is not Trinitarianism but the heresy of modalism, which says that the Trinity is made up of three aspects or *modes* of God, each of which has a different role. But modalism doesn't make sense of passages in Scripture in which the Son is talking to the Father (John 17), saying he will return to the Father (John 14:12, 14:28, 16:10), or that the Son will send the Holy Spirit in his place (John 14:16-17, 14:26, 15:26, 16:13-15; Acts 2:32-33).[53]

The Trinitarian doctrine was not, as some critics assert, a pagan idea that crept into the Church after many centuries. It flowed organically from the early Church Fathers and their understanding of Scripture. Even as early as A.D. 180, before precise language was developed to explain the Trinity, St. Theophilus of Antioch said, "The three days before the luminaries were created are types of the Trinity: God, his Word, and his Wisdom,"[54] which respectively refer to the Father, the Son (John 1:1), and the Holy Spirit (Eph. 1:17). Tertullian wrote in the year 216, "The unity is distributed in a Trinity. Placed in order, the three are the Father, Son, and Spirit."[55]

Although it is a complex mystery ultimately beyond our human reason, the doctrine of the Trinity is not just some theological fine point. In fact, the doctrine demonstrates one of God's most amazing attributes: that he is *love* (1 John 4:8). As love itself, God is a relationship of divine persons: a Trinity of Father, Son, and Holy Spirit who eternally give and receive love. He is not a solitary being who has existed alone from ages past.

17. How do we know that Jesus and the Holy Spirit are divine?

The doctrine that Jesus was (and is) fully God and fully man is called the deity of Christ. It is evident in passages of Scripture in which Jesus spoke with unparalleled authority and made claims that elevated him to the status of God himself. Here are just a few examples:

- In Matthew 11:27, Jesus claims to have an exclusive and absolute relationship with God the Father when he says, "All things have been delivered to me by my Father; and no one knows the Son except the Father, and no one knows the Father except the Son and any one to whom the Son chooses to reveal him."

- In Luke 22:29, Jesus claims to have the authority to confer kingdoms, just like the Father does.

- In John 8:58, Jesus uses the unpronounceable divine name for himself when he says, "before Abraham was, I AM," implying that he existed—eternally—before Abraham lived thousands of years before. This act sent the high priests into a frenzy and motivated them to kill Jesus for blasphemy because he was "making himself equal with God" (John 5:18).

- In John 20:28, Thomas addresses Jesus as "My Lord and my God." Jesus does not correct Thomas for uttering what would have been blasphemy if it were not true.

Some critics object that these references to Jesus' claims of divinity all come from later sources (especially the Gospel of John) and are the product of legendary development. However, even in earlier Gospels such as Mark, there is evidence of Jesus' divine stature. For example, in Mark 2:5, after healing the paralytic, Jesus claims to be able to forgive the man's sins, something that only God has the authority to do. In Mark 6:7, Jesus gathers twelve disciples, which is symbolic of the twelve tribes of Israel. Rather than representing one of the tribes himself, such as the tribe of Levi, which had a claim to the priesthood, Jesus stands apart from the Twelve and gathers them together in the same way that God called the twelve tribes of Israel.

Along with the evidence from the Gospels, the letters in the New Testament confirm that the first Christians worshipped Jesus as God and did not think of him as just a wise human being. They say that Jesus Christ is the "image of the invisible God" (Col. 1:15), in whom the "fullness of deity dwells bodily" (Col. 2:8–9). Jesus has the "form of God" and a name to which every knee shall bend (Phil. 2:6, 10). Finally, Jesus is "our great God and Savior" (Titus 2:13).

The Christians who came after the apostles also recognized that Jesus is God. St. Ignatius of Antioch, in the year A.D. 110, referred to "the Church beloved and enlightened after the love of Jesus Christ, *our God*, by the will of him that has willed everything which is."[56] Ignatius also taught that the Father never made the Son but that both the Son and the Father are equally eternal and equally divine. He wrote, "Jesus Christ . . . was with the Father before the beginning of time, and in the end was revealed."[57]

Likewise the divinity of the Holy Spirit. The Bible says that the Holy Spirit will guide us "into all the truth" (John 16:13), and that it alone comprehends the thoughts of God (1 Cor. 2:11). Who else but God can know all truth or comprehend God's thoughts? In fact, St. Peter shows us the Holy Spirit is God when he asks Ananias, who lied and held back money due to the apostles, "Ananias, why has Satan filled your heart to lie to the Holy Spirit and to keep back part of the proceeds of the land? . . . How is it that you have contrived this deed in your heart? You have not lied to men but to God" (Acts 5:3–4). Not only is the Holy Spirit a person who can be lied to, but lying to the Holy Spirit is the same as lying to God, because the Holy Spirit is the third person of the Holy Trinity.

18. How is it possible for God to become a man?

The mystery of the Incarnation, or the mystery of God's becoming man, is not something that can easily be understood by finite human minds. However, just as we can't fully comprehend God himself but can at least understand him at a certain elementary level, so can we also have a basic understanding of how it is not logically impossible for God to become man in the divine person of Jesus Christ.

As we have already seen, Christians believe that God is a Trinity of Father, Son, and Holy Spirit, who each fully possess the divine nature. Upon his Incarnation, God the Son became man within the body of his mother, Mary. He did all this while remaining one divine person and retaining his fully divine nature, even as he took on a fully human nature through the Incarnation. This mystery is called the *hypostatic union*, and it means that Jesus was not half God and half man (like a Greek demigod) but was 100 percent God and 100 percent man. How is this possible? According to the *Catechism*:

> Christ's human nature belongs, as his own, to the divine person of the Son of God, who assumed it. Everything that Christ is and does in this nature derives from "one of the Trinity." The Son of God therefore communicates to his humanity his own personal mode of existence in the Trinity. In his soul as in his body, Christ thus expresses humanly the divine ways of the Trinity (CCC 470).

Saying that "Jesus is God" means that Jesus is a divine person. Whatever is true of Jesus is also true of God, even if it may sound strange at first. For example, since

Jesus died on the cross, it is also true that God died on the cross, because Jesus is God. Of course, God did not *go out of existence*, but that is not what it means to die.

Death occurs when a being's parts are separated into their basic elements. In this case, Jesus' soul was separated from his body, but God still raised Jesus from the dead (Rom. 10:9). Since Jesus is God, then it is true that Jesus raised himself from the dead, just as he said he would in John 2:19–21.

The *Catechism* goes on to say that even though Christ had a divine nature, his knowledge was true human knowledge; as such, it was limited, and Jesus had to go through a process of learning to acquire it (CCC 472). This is echoed in Luke 2:52, where it says that "Jesus increased in wisdom and in stature, and in favor with God and man." Christ had human knowledge and a human will that cooperated with the Father, but he also possessed a divine will and divine knowledge as a part of his divine nature.

The universe continued to function while Christ was an infant because even though the Son's divine nature was united to his human nature,[58] it was not limited by it. In his divine nature, God the Son continued to operate in perfect communion with the other two divine persons of the Holy Trinity. So it is accurate to say that God, in the person of the Son, became a little baby by taking on a human nature. This doesn't mean, however, that a little baby possessing only a human nature was put in charge of ordering the universe. Instead, God the Son, who was fully divine throughout his entire human life on earth, sustained and still sustains, all of existence.

19. What are some common errors about the Incarnation?

One of the core truths of Christianity is that God the Son was begotten, not made, one in being with the Father, was incarnate of the Virgin Mary, suffered, died, and rose from the dead. Unfortunately, many heresies developed over the centuries that deny some of these basic truths about Christ. Here are the most well-known:

Adoptionism: This is the view that Jesus Christ was a mere human being whom God adopted and upon whom he bestowed a special divine status (generally thought to occur at Jesus' baptism). Pope Victor I condemned Adoptionism as heretical at the end of the second century.

Docetism: This second-century heresy claimed that Jesus was fully God but that his humanity was an illusion. Gnostics, or heretics who believed the body was evil and that matter in general was to be avoided, held this view because they could not tolerate the notion of an embodied savior. But Docetism is refuted by scriptural passages that describe Christ's suffering and death as well as his burial and Resurrection. It was condemned at the ecumenical council of Nicaea in 325, which is why the Nicene Creed says that we believe Jesus "suffered death and was buried."

Arianism: This fourth-century heresy claimed that Jesus was *like* God the Father but was not of the same substance as the Father (meaning that Jesus wasn't God, but merely God's greatest creation). Arians defended this view by citing passages such as Colossians 1:15, which says of Christ, "He is the image of the invisible God, *the first-born* of all creation" [emphasis added]. But these passages only show that Jesus has a special authority and relationship with the Father, not that he is a created being.

The title "first-born of creation" doesn't mean that Jesus was created first and then the rest of creation was made after him. It means that Jesus inherits all of creation and has dominion over it, just as in many cultures in human history a first-born human son has rights over his father's property. The very next verse in Colossians explicitly says that Jesus created "all things," which means Jesus can't be a part of God's creation but must instead be the true God who created all things.

Like Docetism, Arianism was condemned at the ecumenical council of Nicaea and again at the Council of Constantinople in 381. This is why the Nicene Creed says that Jesus is "God from God, Light from Light, true God from true God, begotten, not made, consubstantial [of the same substance] with the Father; through him all things were made.

Nestorianism: This heresy holds that Christ is not one person but two, God the Son and Jesus Christ. It came from a bishop named Nestorius, who believed that Mary was not the Mother of God, but only the mother of the human Christ (he called Mary the "Christ-bearer," or *Christotokos*, and not the "God-bearer," or *Theotokos*).

According to Nestorians, Mary gave Jesus his human nature but God the Father gave Jesus his divine nature, and so Mary can only be thought of as the mother of Christ, not the Mother of God. Now, it's true that Mary is not the source of Christ's divinity, but mothers give birth to *persons*, not natures. If Jesus is God, and Mary is his mother, then it follows that Mary, in the words of St. Irenaeus in the second century, "bore God," and is the *Theotokos*, the Mother of God.[59]

Nestorianism was officially condemned at the ecumenical councils of Ephesus in 431 and Chalcedon in 451, which reaffirmed that Christ is one divine person with a fully human nature and a fully divine nature.

Monophysitism: In contrast to Nestorianism, this heresy correctly taught that Christ is one person, but it erred in teaching that Christ only has one (*mono*) human-divine nature (*physis*). This contradicts the traditional teaching of the hypostatic union that Jesus is one person with two natures, one fully human, which "grew in wisdom and understanding," and the other fully divine, which provided an adequate atonement

for sin. The Council of Chalcedon condemned Monophysitism in 451.

Monothelitism: This is the view that Jesus had only
one will. But since Christ has two natures, it follows
that he has two wills, one human and the other divine.
This is evidenced in the agony in the garden, where
Jesus' human will not to be tortured stands next to his
divine will as both follow the Father's providential decree. Jesus said, "if it be possible, let this cup pass from
me; yet, not as I will, but as thou wilt" (Matt. 26:39).
This heresy was formally condemned at the Third
Council of Constantinople in 681.

20. How can I know that God loves me?

The greatest sign God has given of his love for us was
the sacrifice of his son Jesus Christ on the cross in order to take away the sins of the world. But why did
Jesus, the God-man, choose to die on a cross?

Deep down we all know we are guilty of breaking
God's laws. Although we are made in his image, we
have tarnished that image either by doing wrong or by
failing to do good. Because God is holy, perfect, and
pure, sin is completely destroyed in his presence. Unless we are "made right with God" we cannot expect
to spend eternity with him in heaven, because sins
against God are sins against an infinitely holy being,
and thus would deserve infinite punishment.

But God sent his Son to make an infinite atonement, or reconciliation between God and man, in order to remedy the injustice that our sins have caused. On the cross, Christ represents all of humanity and makes an act of self-sacrifice, an act of perfect love, that redeems all sins at all times in all places.

God certainly could have forgiven our sins through a divine decree (he is omnipotent, after all), but St. Thomas Aquinas argues that Christ's sacrifice was a "fitting" thing for God to do. He said it clearly demonstrated God's love for human beings and provided us with an example of virtue and self-sacrifice.[60] Christ's obedient death also restored the covenant that Adam broke when he disobeyed God in the Garden of Eden.[61]

1 John 2:1–2 says, "If anyone does sin, we have an advocate with the Father, Jesus Christ the righteous; and he is the expiation for our sins, and not for ours only but also for the sins of the whole world." Jesus' death does not merely cause God to ignore or turn away from our sins. It truly *expiates*, or wipes out, our sin and restores us to a living relationship with God as his adopted children (Rom. 8:15). As the *Catechism* puts it:

Jesus did not experience reprobation as if he himself had sinned. But in the redeeming love that always united him to the Father, he assumed us in the state of our waywardness of sin, to the point that he could say in our name from the cross: "My God, my God, why have you forsaken me?" Having thus established him in solidarity with us sinners, God "did not spare his own Son but gave him up for us all," so that we might be "reconciled to God by the death of his Son." By giving up his own Son for our sins, God manifests that his plan for us is one of benevolent love, prior to any merit on our part: "In this is love, not that we loved God but that he loved us and sent his Son to be the expiation for our sins." God "shows his love for us in that while we were yet sinners Christ died for us" (CCC 603–604).

About the Author

Trent Horn is an apologist and speaker for Catholic Answers. He specializes in pro-life issues as well as outreach to atheists and agnostics. He holds a master's degree in theology from Franciscan University of Steubenville.

Endnotes

1   *The Baltimore Catechism*, Lesson 2, Question 8, http://www. catholicity.com/baltimore-catechism/ lesson02.html.

2   Acts 17:25, 28.

3   Pope St. John Paul II, General Audience, July 10, 1985.

4   A variant of polytheism is henotheism, which acknowledges the existence of many gods but only deems one god worthy of worship and obedience.

5   "Their purpose was the persuasion of the masses and general legis-lative and political expediency. For instance, the myths tell us that these gods are anthropomorphic or resemble some of the other animals." Aristotle, *The Metaphysics* (New York: Penguin Books, 1998), 380.

6   St. Thomas Aquinas, *Summa Theologica* I.11.3.

7   Pontifical Council for Culture and the Pontifical Council for Inter-religious Dialogue, "Jesus Christ: The Bearer of the Water of Life: A Christian Reflection on the 'New Age,'" *L'Osservatore Romano*, August 13/20, 2003.

8   C.S. Lewis, *Mere Christianity* (New York: Simon and Schuster, 1952), 152.

9   Christian Smith and Melinda Denton, *Soul Searching: The Reli-gious and Spiritual Lives of American Teenagers* (New York: Ox-ford University Press, 2005), 162–64.

10 St. Anselm, *Anselm of Canterbury: The Major Works*, ed. Brian Da-vies and G.R. Evans (Oxford: Oxford University Press, 2008), 98.

11 *The Shepherd of Hermas* 2:1:1.

12 Process theology has its roots in the thinking of Alfred North

Whitehead (1861–1947). A brief summary can be found in Alister McGrath, *Christian Theology: An Introduction*, 5th edition (West Sussex, England: Wiley-Blackwell, 2011), 214–15.

13 Tatian the Syrian, *Address to the Greeks* 4.

14 St. Augustine, *City of God* V.10.

15 St. Thomas Aquinas, *Summa Theologica* III.1.3.

16 St. Thomas Aquinas, *Summa Contra Gentiles* 1:64.

17 Stephen Hawking and Leonard Mlodinow, *The Grand Design* (New York: Random House, 2010), 1.

18 Derek Parfit, *On What Matters: Volume Two* (Oxford: Oxford University Press, 2011), 27.

19 Richard Taylor, *Metaphysics*, 4th ed. (Englewood Cliffs, N.J.: Prentice-Hall, 1991), 100–1.

20 For more information see John Farrell, *The Day Without Yesterday: Lemaître, Einstein, and the Birth of Modern Cosmology* (New York: Thunder's Mouth Press, 2005), 115. Farrell cautiously notes that, "There is some confusion as to the extent of Einstein's enthusiasm for Lemaître's primeval atom theory . . . Encouraging as Einstein was, it's unlikely that he regarded Lemaitre's primeval atom theory as the last word on the subject—and unlikelier still that he would have employed the word 'creation' to describe it."

21 Although the standard model is still the majority view, it is incomplete. Scientists have proposed new mechanisms such as "inflation" to account for irregularities in the standard model, such as the flatness problem or the horizon problem. Scientists also need a quantum theory of gravity to account for the universe's structure at the Big Bang itself, because relativity theory becomes incapable of describing the singularity prior to what is called the Planck

time, or 10^{-43} seconds. For a more thorough treatment of this subject see the "Advanced cosmology" appendix in my book *Answering Atheism* (2013), published by Catholic Answers Press.

22 Lisa Grossman, "Why Physicists Can't Avoid a Creation Event," *New Scientist*, January 11, 2012. In their original paper, Audrey Mithani and Alexander Vilenkin wrote: "Did the universe have a beginning? At this point, it seems that the answer to this question is probably yes." Mithani and Vilenkin, "Did the Universe Have a Beginning?" Cornell University Library, High Energy Physics-Theory, 2012, http://arxiv.org/abs/1204.4658.

23 Martin Rees, *Just Six Numbers: The Deep Forces That Shape the Universe* (New York: Basic Books, 2000), 10.

24 The phrase was first expressed in Book I of the Roman philosopher Titus Lucretius's work *De Rerum Natura*.

25 John Locke, *An Essay Concerning Human Understanding*, IV.X.3.

26 David Albert, "On the Origin of Everything: 'A Universe from Nothing' by Lawrence M. Krauss," *New York Times Book Review*, March 23, 2012.

27 See Robert J. Spitzer, *New Proofs for the Existence of God: Contributions from Contemporary Physics and Philosophy* (Grand Rapids, Mich.: Wm. B. Eerdmans Publishing, 2010), 27.

28 I am using the word "prior" in this sentence to mean logical priority and not temporal priority, because obviously there was no moment "prior" to the first moment of time and space.

29 Fourth Lateran Council, Decree 1.

30 *The Shepherd of Hermas* 2:1:1.

31 St. Theophilus of Antioch, *To Autolycus* 2:10.

32 Pope Benedict XVI, "Meeting of the Holy Father Benedict

XVI with the Clergy of the Dioceses of Belluno-Feltre and Treviso," July 24, 2007, http://www.vatican.va/holy_father/benedict_xvi/ speeches/2007/july/documents/hf_ben-xvi_spe_20070724_clero-cadore_en.html.

33 Pope Pius XII, *Humani Generis*, 38.

34 See canons 1–5 of the First Vatican Council (1870) and Pope Pius XII, *Humani Generis* (1950).

35 Rees, *Just Six Numbers*, 33–34.

36 "Gravity Mysteries: Why Is Gravity Fine-Tuned?" *New Scientist*, Issue 2712, June 10, 2009, http:// www.newscientist.com/article/mg20227123.000-gravity-mysteries-why-is-gravity-finetuned.html.

37 Alexander Vilenkin, *Many Worlds in One* (New York: Hill and Wang, 2006), 10.

38 Lisa Dyson, Matthew Kleban, and Leonard Susskind, "Disturbing Implications of a Cosmological Constant," Cornell University Library, High Energy Physics-Theory, 2002, http://arxiv.org/abs/hep-th/0208013.

39 Assume for simplicity that the odds of getting a royal flush are one in a million (it's closer to one in 650,000). The odds of getting fifty royal flushes in a row would be one in $(10^6)^{50}$, which leave us with one in 10^{300}. This comes nowhere near Penrose's number for the odds of a low-entropy or extremely well ordered universe (one in 10^{1230}), and is less than the odds of the five other constants and conditions being added together.

40 Paul Davies, "Stephen Hawking's Big Bang Gaps," *Guardian,* September 3, 2010, http://www.guardian.co.uk/commentisfree/belief/2010/sep/04/ stephen-hawking-big-bang-gap.

41 St. Irenaeus, *Against Heresies* 2:13:3.

42 Peter J. Kreeft and Ronald K. Tacelli, *Handbook of Catholic Apologetics: Reasoned Answers to Questions of Faith* (San Francisco: Ignatius Press, 2009), 104.

43 Patrick Lee, "Does God Have Emotions?," in *God Under Fire*, eds. Douglas Huffman and Eric L. Johnson (Grand Rapids, Mich.: Zondervan, 2002), 229–30.

44 St. John Chrysostom, *On the Incomprehensibility of God*, III, 3, 722/200, cited in Stephen Benin, *The Footprints of God: Divine Accommodation in Jewish and Christian Thought* (Albany, N.Y.: SUNY Press, 1993), 68.

45 Joseph Smith Jr., "The King Follett Sermon," *Ensign*, May 1971, 13, https://www.lds.org/ensign/1971/04/the-king-follett-sermon?lang=eng.

46 St. Ignatius of Antioch, *Letter to the Magnesians* 8:1.

47 St. Athanasius, *De Incarnatione* I.

48 Jaroslav Pelikan, *Christianity and Classical Culture: The Metamorphosis of Natural Theology in the Christian Encounter with Hellenism* (New Haven: Yale University Press, 1995), 318.

49 Buddha is recorded as saying in Sutta 11.5 of the *Digha Nikaya*, "Seeing the danger of such miracles, I dislike, reject and despise them." Sura 13:7 of the Qu'ran says, "Those who disbelieved say, 'Why has a sign not been sent down to him from his Lord?' You are only a warner, and for every people is a guide." Muhammad's role was simply to preach about Allah, not to perform miracles.

50 For example, in Acts 2 Peter declares that King David's tomb is still in existence and David has suffered decay, but Jesus as the Messiah has not suffered decay because he was resurrected.

51 "For even his brethren did not believe in him" (John 7:5).

52 According to the *Catechism*, "Because it does not divide the divine unity, the real distinction of the persons from one another resides solely in the relationships which relate them to one another . . . Because of that unity the Father is wholly in the Son and wholly in the Holy Spirit; the Son is wholly in the Father and wholly in the Holy Spirit; the Holy Spirit is wholly in the Father and wholly in the Son" (CCC 255). For a more in-depth discussion see Joseph Ratzinger, *Introduction to Christianity* (San Francisco: Ignatius Press, 1990), 183; and St. Augustine, *On the Trinity*.

53 The *Catechism* says that "'Father,' 'Son,' and 'Holy Spirit' are not simply names designating modalities of the divine being, for they are really distinct from one another" (CCC 254).

54 St. Theophilus of Antioch, *To Autolycus* 2:15.

55 Tertullian, *Against Praxeas* 2.

56 St. Ignatius, *Letter to the Ephesians*, 1.

57 St. Ignatius, *Letter to the Magnesians*, 6.

58 As the Council of Chalcedon (451) defined the union: "without confusion, without change, without division, without separation."

59 St. Irenaeus, *Against Heresies* 5:19:1.

60 St. Thomas Aquinas, *Summa Theologica* III.46.

61 See Romans 5:19.

Become part of the team.
Help support Catholic Answers.

Catholic Answers is an apostolate dedicated to serving Christ by bringing the fullness of Catholic truth to the world. We help good Catholics become better Catholics, bring former Catholics "home," and lead non-Catholics into the fullness of the Faith.

Catholic Answers neither asks for nor receives financial support from any diocese. The majority of its annual income is in the form of donations from individual supporters like you.

To make a donation by phone using your credit card, please speak with one of our customer service representatives at 888-291-8000.

To make a donation by check, please send a check payable to "Catholic Answers" to:

> Catholic Answers
> 2020 Gillespie Way
> El Cajon, CA 92020

To make a donation online, visit **catholic.com**.

catholic.com